# How Forgiveness Works

## Jonathan Baker

Assistant Curate, Sanderstead Team Ministry

**GROVE BOOKS LIMITED**
BRAMCOTE NOTTINGHAM NG9 3DS

# Contents

**Acknowledgements**

I would like to note my thanks to members of the Grove Spirituality Group, for their helpful suggestions and encouragement, and especially to Sue, who typed and soothed.

**The Cover Illustration** is derived from the design on a 12th-century font at Eardisley, Herefordshire

**First Impression** June 1995
**ISSN** 0262-799X
**ISBN** 1 85174 291 3

# 1

# Introduction

Forgiveness is still an everyday word, and roams at large outside the ghetto of theological jargon. It is a dangerous word, at once familiar and mysterious, comforting and subversive. We talk about it lightly, we say 'Sorry' to each other every day, we think we know what it means, until suddenly we are confronted with a profound need either to ask for forgiveness or to offer it to another—then it becomes elusive and disturbing. 'Nothing is less obvious than forgiveness,' is the verdict of one authority.[1] Yet at the same time it can take us right to the heart of the Christian faith and of human experience.

When we see people forgiving each other, overcoming deep injury and outrage in order to do so, it can be striking and memorable. Who could fail to be moved by the words of Gordon Wilson, in the aftermath of the bombing of the Remembrance Day parade at Enniskillen in 1987, publicly tendering forgiveness to those who killed his daughter? By contrast, who could fail to be troubled by the dilemma of the Jewish nation after the Holocaust, expressed on the 50th anniversary of the liberation of Auschwitz by the President of Israel as he said, 'We do not hate, but neither do we forgive'?

Such statements underline the fact that forgiveness is, by its very nature, controversial. This has always been so. Bede records an early example from the mid-7th century AD of the devout King Sigbert of the East Saxons, 'who was murdered by his own kinsmen...who, on being asked their motive, had no answer to make except that they hated the king because he was too lenient towards his enemies and too readily forgave injuries when offenders asked pardon.'[2]

Precisely because forgiveness is such an important and controversial word, it is perhaps presumptuous to try and consider it usefully in a booklet of this size. I have tried to give a simple outline of how forgiveness works, focussing especially upon the way human expressions of forgiveness need to reflect the divine pattern as it is revealed to us in Christ. In the nature of the case forgiveness cannot tidily be restricted to our relationship with God, but keeps on spilling over into our relationships with others. It is on this area of overlap that I have tried to concentrate my attention.

1   E Brunner, *The Mediator* (London: Lutterworth Press, 1934) p 488.
2   Bede, *A History of the English Church and People* (Harmondsworth: Penguin, 1955) p 179.

## 2
# The Problem of Forgiveness

Not everyone sees forgiveness as necessary or even desirable. Some have suggested that forgiveness is at best irrelevant to the quest for human wholeness, and is at worst an immoral refusal to take evil actions seriously. As we try to identify the real quality of Christian forgiveness, it may be helpful to clarify some of the negative or inadequate ways in which the word is commonly used.

For many people, forgiveness can only be offered where the grievance has not been deeply felt. It applies in situations where we can say, 'I do not feel angry and resentful towards you, even though you have done me harm.' At a subjective emotional level the offence has simply not made an impact and has left no scars. It is assumed that forgiving must involve forgetting.

This explains why people can talk about the possibility of forgiveness on an everyday basis, and expect to experience it, while at the same time finding its prospect scandalous and upsetting in more serious situations. When I step on your toe you say, 'It is all right, I forgive you.' What you really mean is, 'It is all right, I was not hurt.' The offence was trivial, and forgiveness in this context is simply an expression of good manners. But if we suggest that forgiveness is an appropriate response to serious and malicious hurt, many will find this outrageous, not least because it implies that the offence was unimportant and did not really matter.

Many Christians are crippled by guilt because they share this inadequate understanding of forgiveness. They believe that they should be willing to forgive others, and that God's ability to forgive them is bound up with their willingness to forgive others. But they cannot bring themselves to forgive because to do so would imply that the injury somehow did not matter. The hurt they have suffered is compounded by a sense of guilt and inadequacy because they feel they cannot be real Christians. Often those who say, 'I could never forgive him for what he did,' are simply stating that they cannot imagine their strong feelings of hurt or bitterness ever subsiding.

### Forgiveness and Denial
For some, forgiveness is a dangerous concept precisely because it suggests to them a reluctance to acknowledge the extent to which someone has been hurt. It implies repressing those feelings of anger and pain and resentment which need to come to the surface if there is to be any genuine healing. So when you deliberately and malevolently stamp on my toe, and I say, 'It is all right, I forgive you,' I am failing to acknowledge that our relationship has

4

gone seriously wrong and I am denying the existence of problems which need to be dealt with.

Far from being a means of establishing acceptance and wholeness and reconciliation, such forgiveness avoids having to face up to the offender honestly. It involves ducking the seriousness of the situation, perhaps because it is too painful to come to terms with, and forgiveness becomes a dishonest shield behind which the victim can retreat in order to avoid facing up to what has gone wrong.

It would appear that much modern psychology takes this view of forgiveness as denial. The late Bishop Stephen Neill used to say that whenever he came across a book on psychology he would always turn to the index to see if there was an entry under 'forgiveness.' It was invariably absent, a fact which he found most disturbing. Part of the reason for this absence is that modern consciences tend to be untroubled by sin and guilt. We worry about our low self-esteem, our inadequacies and insecurities, our feelings of alienation, but it never occurs to us that such feelings might be more than mere illusion, that we might actually be morally responsible for our own disorientation. If the connection between sin and self-esteem were recognized, forgiveness would be much more fashionable, not least because it offers healing for our relationships and thus for our self-image, which depends so much upon our ability to trust and to bond.

## The Right to Forgive

The charge of unreality can be made at a moral level as well as a psychological one. In the first place forgiveness is said to be a moral impossibility because the past cannot be changed; what's done is done and cannot be undone, and whatever actions and events we may lament and regret, they are locked away in the past, beyond our reach and inaccessible. So when I stamp on your toe, the pain is real and unrelieved, and my guilt is fixed and irremovable, whatever form your reaction might take. Forgiveness is therefore pointless, and changes nothing. However, as I hope we shall see, Christian forgiveness is in fact a creative process which not only breaks us free from the destructive grip of the past, but creatively uses the rubble of past failure as the foundation for a wholly new set of opportunities.

In the second place, there is the objection that an individual wishing to offer forgiveness may not have any right to do so, because often there is more than one person affected. It is repeatedly said, for example, that the survivors of the Holocaust are not in a position to forgive their tormentors because they have no right to forgive on behalf of those who died. The dilemma has been expressed by Simon Wiesenthal, the hunter of Nazi war criminals; in 1942 he was summoned to the deathbed of an SS officer who wanted to receive the forgiveness of a Jew before he died. Even though he believed the man was genuinely sorry, Wiesenthal refused, on the grounds that he was simply not in a position to do what was asked of him:

'What would have given me the right,' he asks, 'to forgive on behalf of those whom I had watched die?'[3]

The problem was explored by Dostoevsky in *The Brothers Karamazov* when Ivan Karamazov argues that a mother who witnesses the horrifying murder of her child may be able to forgive the suffering caused to herself, but she cannot forgive on behalf of the child, and to that extent the crime must remain unabsolved. But the response of Ivan's brother Aloysha is a genuinely Christian answer:

'You said just now, is there a being in the whole world who could or had the right to forgive? But there is such a being, and he can forgive everything, everyone and everything, and for everything, because he gave his innocent blood for all and for everything.'[4]

The death and resurrection of Christ is not just a moment in history, of limited importance; it is of universal significance, and has the capacity not only to bring about forgiveness for and between people, but also to make good the inadequacies and limitations of human forgiveness.

Perhaps the most serious objection to the whole notion of forgiveness is not that it is a moral impossibility, but that it is actually immoral, because it appears to disregard ethical norms. If any act, however brutal and selfish, can be redeemed by forgiveness, then the distinction between right and wrong is threatened and justice itself is subverted. We have turned full circle, and are back at our original objection, that forgiveness in the end does not take wrongdoing seriously enough. An emphasis on forgiveness can appear to make wrongdoing acceptable or even desirable, if its consequences can be avoided and all made well again. This is the view implicit in the cynical remark attributed to the philosopher Heinrich Heine on his deathbed: 'God will forgive me—that is his business.'

It is a charge that is as old as the gospel itself, and was made against St Paul: 'What shall we then say? Shall we go on sinning, so that grace may increase?' (Romans 6.1). The apostle thinks not, and as we turn to consider the way forgiveness actually works, we shall begin to see why.

---

**3** Quoted in M Hubaut, *Forgiveness* (Middlegreen: St Paul's, 1994) p 13.
**4** F Dostoevsky, *The Brothers Karamazov* (Harmondsworth: Penguin, 1958) p 288.

# 3

# *The Foundation of Forgiveness*

Bishop Lesslie Newbigin tells the story of how, as a young missionary in India, he went to classes with a teacher of the theistic form of Hinduism (sometimes called India's theology of grace). On one occasion the teacher asked Newbigin what he meant by salvation; Newbigin gave his answer in terms of sin and forgiveness, upon which the Hindu remarked that 'apart from the personal name of Jesus, what you have said is exactly what I would have said.' 'If that is so,' Newbigin asked, 'what is the basis for your confidence that your sins are forgiven?' 'If God would not forgive my sins,' came the reply, 'I would go to a god who would.'[5]

The story is shocking to Christian ears not just because of the idea that there might be more than one God, but because of the way forgiveness is made a quality detachable from God's character. In the Old Testament it is clear that forgiveness is deeply rooted in the character of God; it is not negotiable. Forgiveness is repeatedly linked to the very name of Yahweh. 'For the sake of your name, O Yahweh,' cries the Psalmist, 'forgive my iniquity, though it is great' (Psalm 25.11). Forgiveness as a central quality of God's very being is embedded in the creeds of Israel. 'You are a forgiving God, gracious and compassionate, slow to anger and abounding in love' (Nehemiah 9.17).

Here we find the reason why divine and human forgiveness are so closely related. If humankind is made in the image of God, then the ability to forgive is essential for a full and rounded human life, because it reflects the attitude of God himself. By contrast, unforgiveness can lead to an impaired life because it implies estrangement from God.

A further point illustrated by Lesslie Newbigin's story is that Christian forgiveness is not a response to the need of sinners to feel good about themselves. The Hindu's point is that a god should be selected on the basis of his ability to meet our need as sinners, for which purpose forgiveness is a useful quality for a god to have. But in Christian understanding, the problem is how to repair broken relationships with this particular God and with particular people. The key words in Christianity are relational words: faith, love, forgiveness. The process of forgiveness is not for the benefit of the sinner alone, but always aims at restoring fellowship.

Yet the question remains, on what basis does God forgive? 'Does something *happen* for forgiveness? Or is it just a word?' asks one of Iris Murdoch's

---

**5**   Bishop Newbigin told this story during questions following a talk 'Why Christianity and not another philosophy?' at Croydon Parish Church, 21st February 1994.

characters in her novel *Bruno's Dream*. The question implies that some sort of event is necessary, and Christians naturally see such an event in the death and resurrection of Christ.

Nevertheless, this has been questioned. 'How miserably all those finely constructed theories of sacrifice and vicarious atonement crumble to pieces before this faith in the love of God our Father, who so gladly pardons! The one parable of the Prodigal Son wipes them all off the slate.'[6] The father of the prodigal simply forgives, out of his own generosity of heart; the parable contains no plausible reference to anything equivalent to the cross (despite the suggestion that in a Middle Eastern culture the father's loss of dignity in running to meet his son is suggestive of the cross).[7]

Such a view comes perilously close to the superficial understandings of forgiveness examined in the previous section. The parable of the prodigal illustrates the compassion of God but does not explore the basis of forgiveness. Something decisive and objective must underlie our concept of forgiveness if it is to have any real transforming power. 'Can't you forgive me?' implores the adulterous central character in Tom Wolfe's novel, *Bonfire of the Vanities*. 'I suppose I could,' replies his wife. 'But what would that change?'[8] Forgiveness is not some abstract pardon; it is the process by which a broken relationship is creatively restored and once again made healthy and life-giving for both sides. Such a transformation does not take place simply by uttering the magic words, 'I forgive you.' Something more than that is needed.

### Forgiveness in the Old Testament

The Old Testament itself finds the notion of forgiveness problematic, not because it might be too easy and superficial, but because it seems impossible. From earliest times the Hebrews believed sin to have irreversible consequences both for the individual sinner and for the community of which he or she was a part.[9] Sin was not seen as an action distinct from its consequences; it was the beginning of a chain of events which would inexorably lead to disaster for the sinner and his people, even 'to the third and fourth generations.' The sin and its penalty could be spoken of as if they were the same thing, as in Numbers 32.23: 'You may be sure that your sin will find you out.' Furthermore, guilt was real; sin was an objective barrier placing the sinner outside the fellowship of God.

The possibility of forgiveness was therefore limited, at least until the Exile. There were particular difficulties with crimes covered by the Decalogue, such as idolatry (Joshua 24.19) and murder (2 Kings 24.3f). More alarmingly,

6   Paul Wernle, quoted in D M Baillie, *God was in Christ* (London: Faber, 1961) p 172.
7   Kenneth Bailey *Poet and Peasant and Through Peasant Eyes* (Grand Rapids: Eerdmans, 1983)
8   T Wolfe, *The Bonfire of the Vanities* (London: Picador, 1988) p 485.
9   G von Rad, *Old Testament Theology, Vol 1* (London: SCM, 1975) p 264ff.

King Saul could not be forgiven his disobedience in failing to annihilate the Amalekite livestock, even though he begged Samuel to absolve him (1 Samuel 15.24-26).

Yet God is the God of his people and will remain faithful to his covenant promises, which means that the possibility of forgiveness must be present. Even so, forgiveness seems to be quite compatible with the continuation of judgment. At any single moment God may be experienced both as the One who forgives and as the One who avenges wrongdoing, as expressed for example in Psalm 99.8, 'You were to Israel a forgiving God, though you punished their misdeeds.'

The combination of forgiveness and judgment is enshrined in some of Israel's earliest credal statements. For example, 'The Lord is slow to anger and abounding in steadfast love, forgiving iniquity and transgression, but'—and here comes the catch—'he will by no means clear the guilty, visiting the iniquity of fathers upon children, upon the third and upon the fourth generation' (Numbers 14.18-23, echoing Exodus 34.6f).

It is as if the Old Testament writers are acutely aware of two, apparently irreconcilable truths: firstly, that sin is utterly destructive and must be treated by God with absolute seriousness; and secondly, that God is forgiving and will not ultimately allow sin to frustrate his covenant promises. In such circumstances it is far from clear what forgiveness actually means. What can it mean for God to forgive if judgment continues?

Against this background two developments help to resolve the paradox. The first of these was the growth of the sacrificial system, which was intended to provide a way to remove sin and restore fellowship with God.[10] The offering of animal sacrifices to atone for sin dramatically conveyed the reality that the sinner need not inevitably be destroyed by his or her sin. Instead, the destructive consequences of sin were symbolically redirected upon the sacrifice when the worshipper laid hands upon it before killing it. In this way sin could be put to death without destroying the sinner. It made forgiveness possible without winking at sin. Sacrifice dealt with sin vicariously, but not painlessly.

Alongside the development of the sacrificial system there was also a growing emphasis on spiritual sacrifice which identified the sacrifice even more closely with the sinner. 'The sacrifices of God are a broken spirit; a broken and contrite heart, O God, you will not despise' (Psalm 51.17). In their different ways, both understandings of sacrifice stress the seriousness of sin and the costliness of eradicating it.

The second Old Testament development which is relevant was Israel's experience of exile, and her theological response to it. Israel's prophets,

---

**10** L Morris, *The Atonement* (Leicester: IVP, 1983) ch 2.

historians and priests all interpreted the destruction of Jerusalem in 587 BC and the exile which followed as Yahweh's judgment upon his people for the accumulated sins of several centuries. It is as if the destruction of the nation was the only way by which the effects of sin could be exhausted and disarmed and the people brought to repentance.[11]

Israel having been humiliated and rendered powerless, her armies defeated, her cities in ruins, her national institutions destroyed and her ruling class carried off into captivity, the stage was set for forgiveness to be considered. Thus it is that the prophets who speak most clearly of unconditional forgiveness and the grace of God are Jeremiah, Ezekiel and Deutero-Isaiah, all of whom speak from the midst of the ravages of exile. Only from the depths of judgment can the word of forgiveness be spoken, because only in a situation of alienation and exile can sin be put away and repentance be deep and lasting.

### Forgiveness from the Cross

In the New Testament Christ's death is the perfect sacrifice. 'Behold the Lamb of God,' cries John the Baptist, 'who takes away the sins of the world' (John 1.29). The Letter to the Hebrews identifies the blood of Christ as the supreme sin-offering, far surpassing the blood of goats and bulls shed on the Day of Atonement (Hebrews 9.12-14). At the Last Supper Jesus himself interprets his coming death as a sacrifice creating a new relationship with God: 'This is my blood of the covenant, which is poured out for many for the forgiveness of sins' (Matthew 26.28).

Such language makes a clear link between sacrifice, the death of Christ, the forgiveness of sins and reconciliation with God. Christ dies 'for us,' bearing our sins and taking them down into death. He goes as our representative where we cannot go, in order that our sin and guilt may be destroyed in death. In his death he removes the barrier disrupting our fellowship with God, and in his resurrection he opens up the way of forgiveness.

If we then identify ourselves with Christ by repentance and faith, like the Israelite worshippers of old, we find in the death of Christ an effective sacrifice. The entail of sin has been broken, because its destructive inheritance has been vested not upon the sinner but upon Christ. By means of such a sacrifice, God is able to offer forgiveness without sparing the sin. As George MacDonald put it, 'What is usually called "forgiving the sin" means "forgiving the sinner and *destroying* the sin."'[12] Such forgiveness is infinitely costly to God, but completely free for the sinner.

Indeed, all the New Testament evidence underlines the cost of offering

---

**11** See for example Walter Brueggemann *Hopeful Imagination: Prophetic Voices in Exile* (London: SCM, 1986)

**12** C S Lewis (ed) *George MacDonald: An Anthology* (London: Bles, 1946) p 27.

forgiveness as well as the fact that it is free to those who receive it. The parables that use the imagery of debt make this especially clear. The king who cancels his servant's huge debt in Matthew 18 does so at enormous cost to himself. Forgiveness in this story may be free for the servant, but it certainly is not for the king.

Human love instinctively follows the same pattern; for example, the loving parents whose child rejects them do not retaliate in kind. They might feel entitled to cut off all contact and cast the child off, but instead they absorb the child's anger and ingratitude, not throwing it back but taking it upon themselves where it can cause pain to no-one else. Such action is sacrificial; the parents take upon their own shoulders the cause of the estrangement, so that there is no longer any barrier to the relationship. Their attitude is certainly costly, but it allows them to hold out to the child the possibility of forgiveness and reconciliation.

Such forgiveness involves the surrender of what we are morally entitled to. It involves resisting the impulse to pay back our assailants with interest. It involves breaking the cycle (or is it more often a spiral?) of tit-for-tat by accepting the injury done and determining that it shall go no further. In this respect it mirrors the forgiveness offered at Calvary.

### Forgiveness and Forsakenness

The New Testament also picks up the theme of exile. Christ is crucified as King of the Jews and so on the cross he enters the ultimate state of exile on behalf of God's people. Just as the Israelites were unable to receive forgiveness before they had come under judgment and learned repentance in the midst of destruction and exile, so God's final word of forgiveness is not possible apart from the destruction of sin in Christ's body as the representative of his people, setting them free to repent.

It is no accident that the word of forgiveness must be spoken from the cross, which is the place of exile, nor that 'Father, forgive them' (Luke 23.34) is spoken alongside 'My God, why have you forsaken me?' (Mark 15.34), since forgiveness is only possible where there is forsakenness. Sin is sent away into exile on the cross, whilst the exiles are set free to return to God.

Crucified between criminals, Jesus was indeed 'numbered with the transgressors' and died the death of a runaway slave or a violent terrorist. Yet by identifying with exiles in his death, one of them is moved to faith, and Jesus is able to promise him, 'Today you will be with me in paradise' (Luke 23.43). By entering exile with his people, the Messiah is able to bring that exile to an end.

The story of Zacchaeus in Luke 19 illustrates this well. Zacchaeus is a 'sinner'; not only is his trade likely to involve dishonesty and extortion, but as a tax collector he is effectively working for the enemies of God's people.

He is apparently quite beyond the pale of God's favour. By going to Zacchaeus' house and sharing a meal with him, Jesus should have become tainted with Zacchaeus' sin. But in fact the opposite happens and instead of Jesus becoming an outcast, Zacchaeus is declared to be a true Israelite, no longer a sinner and no longer exiled. This is the meaning of Jesus' declaration, 'Today salvation has come to this house, because this man, too, is a son of Abraham.' Jesus has entered Zacchaeus' exile in order to identify with him in his sin and move him to repentance.

The New Testament of course interprets the cross of Christ in other ways besides those of sacrifice and exile. St Paul in particular speaks little of forgiveness as such, but his treatment of justification and righteousness amounts to the same thing, namely the reconciling of sinners to God.[13] In all these different approaches to forgiveness three things are clear and consistent. In the first place, forgiveness is offered to us freely and unconditionally; it is God's gift and can only be received as such. In the second place, forgiveness is a gift which is immeasurably costly for God to provide. And finally, it is a gift which prompts a response. To this we shall shortly turn.

### The Pattern of Forgiveness

We have focused on the biblical material because it is here that we see what authentic forgiveness consists of, in contrast to the counterfeits considered earlier. The cross of Christ is constitutive not just of our experience of God's forgiveness, but also of our understanding of what forgiveness actually is. By pondering God's forgiveness we begin to understand what the word means, and there we find a pattern which human forgiveness must follow. As Mackintosh puts it, 'Let the man be found who has undergone the shattering experience of pardoning, nobly and tenderly, some awful wrong to himself, still more to one beloved by him, and he will understand the meaning of Calvary better than all the theologians in the world.'[14]

The cross also shows that forgiveness is more than an attitude in the mind of God; it demonstrates that genuine forgiveness involves action. The journey into exile is a journey with a purpose—not merely to offer forgiveness, but to establish it. The risen Christ returns from exile not alone, but leading the exiles home. Hence God's purpose is to offer forgiveness creatively, so that the offender is enabled to respond with repentance and faith. Forgiveness is therefore not a one-off event, but involves a process, a journey—what Mackintosh calls 'voyages of anguish.'[15]

From this we begin to get a picture of forgiveness as something that flows

---

**13** H Vorlander, 'Forgiveness' in C Brown (ed.) *Dictionary of New Testament Theology, Vol 1* (Exeter: Paternoster, 1975) p 702.
**14** H R Mackintosh, *The Christian Experience of Forgiveness* (London: Nisbet, 1927) p 191.
**15** *Ibid*, p 188.

outwards from the heart of God. It is a missionary impulse, and is expressed both concretely and cosmically at Calvary; it gives shape and direction to the mission of the church; it refuses to accept that the future must inevitably be determined by failures and omissions made in the past; and it refuses to stop with the recipient, but insists upon breaking the grip of unforgiveness in the hearts of the forgiven. The experience of divine forgiveness leads not only to fellowship with God in Christ, but to a willingness to forgive others, not just in principle but in action.

Of course this does not always happen. E M Forster describes how forgiveness can break down when the recipient refuses to forgive another:

'"Not any more of this!" she cried. "You shall see the connection if it kills you, Henry! You have had a mistress—I forgave you. My sister has a lover—you drive her from the house. Do you see the connection? Stupid, hypocritical, cruel—oh, contemptible!...Men like you use repentance as a blind, so do not repent. Only say to yourself: 'What Helen has done, I have done.'"'[16]

Henry's wilful inability to 'see the connection' drives his wife to the point where she announces, 'I am unable to forgive you and am leaving you,' and so the relationship breaks down totally.[17]

Here perhaps is one of the profoundest problems with forgiveness. Many people are unwilling to receive it, not simply because that would involve the humiliation of acknowledging that they have done wrong in the first place, but also because it would imply having to forgive in return—for in human relationships forgiveness is rarely one-sided but often needs to be mutual. Might it not be that we often refuse to accept forgiveness not because we are convinced that we are in the right but because we cannot bear to pay the price of responding to forgiveness with forgiveness?

'Forgive us our sins as we forgive those who sin against us,' we pray. Yet the Lord's Prayer makes a connection that is radical in its implications. It makes God's willingness to forgive us conditional upon our willingness to forgive others. The two stand or fall together. We cannot find the strength to forgive others unless we have experienced being forgiven for ourselves; neither can we expect to receive forgiveness if we are unwilling to offer it. Such teaching surely makes sense only within the context of the church, where the support of Word and Sacrament and the fellowship of the forgiven gives this teaching about forgiveness concrete expression. It is to this that we now turn.

---

16 E M Forster, *Howards End* (Harmondsworth: Penguin, 1983) p 300.
17 *Ibid*, p 324.

# 4
# *The Acceptance of Forgiveness*

We have considered the quality of forgiveness so that we can tell the genuine article apart from its many counterfeits, and we have looked at the foundation God has laid to make forgiveness possible. Yet the knowledge both that we can recognize forgiveness and that God has made it possible is still not enough to bring it about. Forgiveness must necessarily involve two parties and it makes no difference what extraordinary lengths God may have gone to in order to hold out the hand of forgiveness, if in the end his creatures refuse it.

In human relationships the problem is common enough: what can be done when forgiveness is refused? When this happens it may feel like a personal failure for the one wishing to forgive, and may lead even to a sense of guilt because the relationship cannot be repaired single-handedly. The limitations of one party to establish forgiveness and reconciliation was poignantly brought home by a survivor of the massacres in Rwanda in 1994, who, speaking to a TV news reporter, asked, 'How can we forgive when no-one will admit they have done wrong?' The attitude of those being offered forgiveness is every bit as important as that of those making the offer. Willingness to forgive must be matched by a willingness to be forgiven. What is involved when this happens? How is forgiveness received? And what happens when it is refused?

## The Forgiving Gift

If we look to God in order to gain insight into how forgiveness works, we find that there is a trinitarian quality about it. If the Father is the One with whom we must ultimately be reconciled, and if the Son is the One through whom this is made possible by his death and resurrection, then the Spirit is the One who works to bring about a response in the life of the sinner. It is as if God is present on both sides of the Creator-creature relationship. The Holy Spirit is able to go round the back, as it were, in order that love may respond to Love and the estranged children may be drawn back to their heavenly Father. This means that the balance between God and his creatures is not an equal one; the right of veto enjoyed by human beings in the face of their Creator, though real enough, is circumscribed by the Holy Spirit. When God offers forgiveness it is not left passively on the table as if God then walks away saying, 'Take it or leave it.' The involvement of the Holy Spirit in the work of forgiveness makes it a much more powerful and creative process than we sometimes imagine.

14

The key New Testament passage which explores the relationship between forgiveness and the Holy Spirit is John 20.21ff: 'Again Jesus said, "Peace be with you! As the Father has sent me, I am sending you." And with that he breathed on them and said, "Receive the Holy Spirit. If you forgive any their sins, they are forgiven; if you do not forgive them, they are not forgiven."' The extraordinary implication of this passage is that the trinitarian life of God can be described simply in terms of forgiveness. The Father sends the Son, the Son sends the Spirit, the Spirit empowers the church and the result is forgiveness. This means we can relate forgiveness to the rich activity of God at every level.

In particular, the activity of God in forgiving is continuous with his activity in creating the world in the beginning, and in calling Israel into being as God's new humanity, his creative response to the Fall. The Spirit, or breath, of God broods over the waters of chaos in Genesis 1.1, and responds to the Word of God in creation. Ezekiel, the prophet in exile, has a powerful vision of the Spirit of God breathing new life into the dead bones of God's people, a vision preceded by promises both of forgiveness and of the gift of God's Spirit. Following this Old Testament image of creation and resurrection, it then should come as no surprise to see the risen Christ similarly breathing out God's Spirit in order to recreate the people of God.

The implication is clear. The gift of the Spirit of forgiveness, coming as it does in the context of Christ's resurrection and echoing the imagery of Genesis 1 and Ezekiel 37, is an act of new creation, an act of cosmic power and significance. Forgiveness in this context is no mere retrospective pardoning of sins. It fulfils God's creative purpose. It is an eschatological event, offering us a glimpse of the new heaven and the new earth, like the resurrection itself.

When we forgive each other, we are participating in the resurrection life of Christ. The church as the special creation of the Holy Spirit is charged not only with the task of proclaiming forgiveness, but is especially to embody forgiveness. The church of Christ is to be known as the community of forgiveness within which the end-time promises of reconciliation, healing and peace can become present realities. Those who are forgiven are in turn empowered by the Spirit to forgive others. Hence Peter in his Pentecost sermon is able to say, 'Repent and be baptized, every one of you, in the name of Jesus Christ for the forgiveness of your sins; and you shall receive the gift of the Holy Spirit' (Acts 2.38). The involvement of the Spirit ensures that forgiveness is not a one-off gift, but is a continuing process and a repeated opportunity. In all the emphasis in recent decades on the work of the Holy Spirit, it is remarkable how little has been said about forgiveness as a gift of the Spirit, and as the charismatic movement develops more will need to be said about the link between fresh experiences of the Spirit's power and forgiveness.

## The Community of Forgiveness

The church as the community of forgiveness makes both the experience and the need for forgiveness more visible. It should embody an ethos of forgiveness, an expectation that forgiveness is both necessary and possible, that can encourage both the offer and acceptance of forgiveness. In this way we can speak meaningfully of the Holy Spirit being active on both sides of a human reconciliation as well as when we receive forgiveness from God. Even if there is only one mutual friend between two people who have quarrelled, that may be enough to create the expectation that forgiveness and reconciliation must come about. When forgiveness is given a setting in a community, it is not simply an issue between two individuals. It is something which affects the whole community, and towards which the community can work.

The visible bones of the church are meant to express its true nature. So, for example, the gospel it preaches is 'the knowledge of salvation through the forgiveness of…sins' (Luke 1.77), whilst the sacraments are visible pledges of forgiveness. In the Creed it is no accident that the statement, 'We believe in one holy, catholic and apostolic Church,' is immediately followed by, 'We acknowledge one baptism for the forgiveness of sins.' Calvin noted the appropriateness of this, saying that 'Forgiveness of sins, then, is for us the first entry into the church and kingdom of God. Without it, there is for us no covenant or bond with God.' Having received us into the church, God also 'preserves and protects us there. For what would be the point of providing a pardon for us that was destined to be of no use?…unless we are sustained by the Lord's constant grace in forgiving our sins, we shall scarcely abide one moment in the church.'[18] Here again we see the need for a strong doctrine of the Holy Spirit if we are to grasp the nature of forgiveness as a continuing reality sustaining our fellowship.

The boundary of the church is marked by baptism, which is supremely a sign of forgiveness, of spiritual cleansing, and of the new relationship with God and his people that forgiveness entails. Moreover it is in the waters of baptism that we are united with Christ in his death and resurrection. When Paul answered the accusation that free forgiveness encourages sin, he did so by pointing to baptism. The language of dying and rising with Christ is not meant to be merely figurative, but indicates a real putting to death of sin in the life of the Christian and a real sharing in the resurrection life of Christ. Forgiveness that follows the pattern of baptism (which itself follows the pattern of the cross and resurrection) is not open to the charge of immorality, because it does not allow for 'cheap grace.' The church's orientation is fixed and sustained not only by baptism, but also by the eucharist, as the commu-

---

**18** J Calvin, *Institutes of the Christian Religion, Vol II* (Philadelphia: The Westminster Press, 1960) p 1034f.

nity identifies with Christ in his death and resurrection in the breaking of bread and pouring out of wine, the 'blood of the covenant which is poured out for many for the forgiveness of sins' (Matthew 26.28).

### Celebrating Forgiveness

To the extent that the church is not in practice a community where forgiveness is experienced and expressed, it denies its own nature. At times the church's role as the guardian of public morality has obscured its true gospel identity; it is not a community of the righteous, but of the forgiven. It was a weak doctrine of the Spirit that led the church in the second century to teach that there could be no forgiveness for sins committed after baptism, and especially not for adultery, idolatry or murder.[19] In response to the pastoral problems this caused, the sacrament of penance developed, though for many centuries even that was permissible only once in a lifetime after baptism.

Perhaps the problem with the Word and Sacraments is that they are so multi-faceted that their united witness to the centrality of forgiveness can be obscured. We might consider ways in which our worship and corporate life might celebrate the reality of forgiveness more explicitly. It is a weakness of Cranmer's liturgy, for example, that it expresses so little assurance of forgiveness. Even the Gloria at the end of the Holy Communion service is marked more by its pleas for mercy than by its celebration of reconciliation and new life. Similarly in the modern Rite A Communion service the short Absolution is immediately followed by the Prayer of Humble Access, which effectively undercuts any sustained celebration of the declaration of forgiveness. Yet the celebration of forgiveness should be a hallmark of the church's worship and needs always to be borne in mind by those planning services.

Where there have been particular occasions of forgiveness, it may be appropriate to celebrate them in rites designed for that purpose. For example a rite of penance and forgiveness following a divorce might be held prior to a remarriage, or a rite of penance and restitution following public scandal.[20] One church devised its own moving ceremony for the reconciliation of the sexes as part of a teaching series on sexuality, which enabled members of the congregation to offer each other forgiveness.[21]

### The Politics of Forgiveness

The placing of forgiveness in a community context raises the important question of corporate forgiveness. How can forgiveness work in society? The question is difficult, not least because communities, tribes and nations

---

19  J N D Kelly, *Early Christian Doctrines* (London: A & C Black, 5th ed., 1977) p 198.
20  See the discussion on services of reconciliation of the penitent in Grove Ethical Study 89, Oliver O'Donovan and Michael Vasey *Liturgy and Ethics* (Nottingham: Grove, 1993).
21  This was at Holy Trinity, Coventry, under its then vicar Graham Dow.

rarely express penitence, let alone forgiveness. Yet Christ's forgiveness is political. The cry from the cross, 'Father, forgive them' (Luke 23.34) 'releases his followers from any obligation to avenge him.'[22] Christ's example offers a striking model for politicians. Charles I's 13-year-old daughter Elizabeth recorded her father's words to her the day before his execution. 'He told me he had forgiven all his enemies, and hoped God would forgive them also, and commanded us, and all the rest of my brothers and sisters, to forgive them.'[23] When Charles II was restored to the throne eleven years later his reign was marked more by tolerance than by the settling of old scores.

More recently, when the Italian Vice-President Vittorio Bachelet was murdered by the Red Brigade, his family expressed their forgiveness at the televised funeral. Years later Bachelet's brother received a letter, signed by eighteen imprisoned members of the Red Brigade, saying, 'We want you to come...We remember very well what your nephew said at his father's funeral...that ceremony when life triumphed over death and we, too, were overcome.'[24]

Individual leaders may also represent their people in asking for forgiveness. We may think perhaps of Willy Brandt kneeling before the memorial to the Warsaw ghetto, or the Czechoslovakian president Victor Havel who, in his first statement on foreign policy, asked forgiveness of the German Sudeten minority for their expulsion from Czechoslovakia.[25]

Such gestures cannot be backed with significant action, which limits their value. In contrast, there has been much more talk of forgiveness and reconciliation in South Africa since the dismantling of apartheid than there was before. The political removal of unjust structures acted as a sign of repentance, allowing space for forgiveness to be offered. There, too, people are amazed at the absence of a backlash against the former white rulers. But to have offered forgiveness before would have been to condone the sin, and could neither have succeeded nor been tolerated.

The church as a community clearly has a role in the politics of forgiveness, since by living as a community of reconciliation in a world torn by hatred and division it can act as an effective sign and symbol of another kind of society. Especially potent are communities such as those at Rostrevor and Corrymeela in Northern Ireland, set in the midst of sectarian divisions.

The church also has a role in prompting repentance.[26] When Christians speak out and are willing even to suffer for the truth, society becomes aware

---

22 Una O'Higgins O'Malley, quoted in B Frost, *Women and Forgiveness* (London: Fount, 1990) p 45.
23 M Mayne, preface to B Frost, *ibid.*
24 *Ibid*, p 15.
25 M Hubaut, *op cit*, p 8.
26 The following points follow P Fiddes, *Past Event and Present Salvation* (London: Darton, Longman and Todd, 1989) p 203.

of injustice, and pressure for change can build up. Furthermore, faith and hope in the coming kingdom of God, joyfully expressed in the midst of suffering and oppression, 'exasperates the agents of the system...it destroys their morale.'[27] Finally, suffering for justice keeps alive the hope of liberation in the reformer's heart, so that the desire for peace and justice becomes ever more urgent, and is held ever more tenaciously.

In such ways the Christian enters the exile of the cross and bears the burden of society's sin in order to exhaust its power and bring it to repentance. South Africa stands as an example of where the church has followed this calling. Yet at the same time it must be remembered that reconciliation is the aim, not victory. When a decisive political advantage is gained, the dynamic of forgiveness requires that it should not be over-exploited and turned into an oppressive victory.

Forgiveness can thus express salvation in the broadest sense. Jeremiah makes a connection between forgiveness and social stability, peace and prosperity, and also health and healing (Jeremiah 33.6-9). The same connection is made explicitly in James 5.14-16: 'Confess your sins to each other and pray for each other so that you may be healed.' Both forgiveness and healing are aspects of the Spirit's work of reconciling, healing and bringing to completion the creation which God has begun.

### The Place of Penitence

Forgiveness must be received as well as offered if true reconciliation is to take place. When Gordon Wilson memorably forgave those responsible for his daughter's death in the Enniskillen bombing, the offer was never taken up. There was some expression of regret that Mr. Wilson's daughter should have been killed, but no regret for the planting of the bomb and certainly no sign of repentance. No discussion of forgiveness can be complete without giving some thought to the place of penitence, for this describes the process by which forgiveness is received and blossoms into restored fellowship.

Faith and penitence are two sides of the same coin. Faith draws one into fellowship with God; penitence is faith overcoming the barrier of sin to restore fellowship. The penitent heart is not one deserving of forgiveness; it is simply the sinful heart which is capable of receiving forgiveness. We can therefore say that faith and penitence are alike in this further respect: that they are both received as gifts of grace. There is consequently nothing to be gained by asking whether forgiveness is conditional upon repentance any more than there is by asking if the resurrection of Christ be conditional upon faith. Yet without faith the resurrection is meaningless to the individual, and without repentance forgiveness cannot restore a broken relationship.

---

27  L Boff, quoted in P Fiddes, *ibid*, p 203.

A brief glance at the gospels reveals that Christ does not look for repentance before holding out forgiveness. He does not ask the tax collector Matthew to repent before calling him (Matthew 9.9-13), neither does he tell the sinful woman who anointed his feet to repent (Luke 7.36-50). On the contrary, he assures her unconditionally that her sins are forgiven. What he does say, most significantly, is that it is her faith that has saved her, which suggests that he is aware of the woman's penitent heart and her capacity to receive forgiveness and be restored to fellowship.

The notion that repentance is a gift of God needs to be understood in the context of what was said earlier about the work of the Holy Spirit and the role of the community in forgiveness. Perhaps this makes more sense if we recognize the connection between awareness of God and awareness of self. Calvin argued that 'without knowledge of God there is no knowledge of self'—and vice-versa.[28] Only by measuring ourselves against the perfection of Christ can we gain true self-awareness, and so be moved to repentance.

Such self-knowledge comes to us as a gift. Left to ourselves, we should never be moved to repentance, for 'what man in all the world would not gladly remain as he is…so long as he does not know himself?'[29] Saving knowledge of God and oneself is the gift of the Holy Spirit as he shines upon the dark places of our hearts with the light of Christ. The experience may be described variously (but not exhaustively!) with words like guilt, emptiness, need, alienation, fear and longing. Such knowledge comes most frequently through contact with the lives and witness of Christians in the community of the church.

### Repentance and Grace

The Westminster Shorter Catechism asks the question, 'What is repentance?' 'Repentance unto life,' goes the answer, 'is a saving grace, whereby a sinner, out of a true sense of his sin, and apprehension of the mercy of God in Christ, doth with grief and hatred of his sin turn from it unto God, with full purpose of and endeavour after new obedience.' In other words, repentance involves the whole personality with its intellect, emotions and will. The need for all three modes of consciousness to be involved is succinctly summarized by Mackintosh: 'Recognition of sin by itself is not repentance; it may be defiance. Nor is sorrow for sin repentance, if it be alone in the mind; it may be remorse or despair. Abandonment of sin, by itself, may be no more than prudence. The regenerating fact is all three, as a unity, baptized in a sense of God's personal grace to the sinful.'[30]

The crucial importance of repentance in forgiveness further answers the

---

**28** J Calvin, *op cit*, Vol I, pp 35-38.
**29** *Ibid.*
**30** H R Mackintosh, *op cit*, p 234.

charge that forgiveness is immoral. That charge has already been answered by stressing the need for the sinner, by faith, to identify with Christ crucified, so that, in St Paul's terms, 'I have been crucified with Christ; it is no longer I who live, but Christ who lives in me' (Galatians 2.20). In practical terms, being 'crucified with Christ' means repentance, the putting to death of sin in one's own life. Such repentance must come by grace, or else forgiveness becomes dependent upon our own effort, and is transformed into a work of self-righteousness, whereas the whole point of the gospel is that forgiveness is being offered to sinners and outcasts, with repentance as part of the gift. Grace has power to set the sinner free to repent.

This can also happen in human relationships, where repentance is sometimes drawn forth simply by holding out the hand of forgiveness. Michael Bordeaux tells the story of two prisoners sharing the same cell in the Russian gulag. One was a Baptist Christian, the other an atheist who taunted the Christian and tried to break his faith. On one occasion it seemed that the atheist had nearly succeeded and the Christian was reduced almost to the point of despair and cried out to God for strength. Then, 'suddenly he looked at me and smiled. I was amazed at his face: there was something joyous about it, pure, as though it had just been washed clean. The weight immediately fell from my soul. I understood that he had forgiven me.'[31]

However those offering forgiveness need not feel responsible if it is not accepted. W H Auden, writing about the refusal of Shakespeare's character Antonio to receive forgiveness from Prospero in *The Tempest*, sums up Antonio's position thus:

'Your all is partial, Prospero,
   My will is all my own:
Your need to love shall never know
Me: I am I, Antonio,
   By choice myself alone.'[32]

Conversely, the offer of forgiveness may be met with a false repentance. Antony Bridge gives an example in his autobiography: 'My father's…understandable and in some ways rather endearing habit of confessing to my mother that he had yet again succumbed to an adulterous temptation, while begging her to forgive him, did not help the marriage; for when she did indeed forgive him, he was able to go happily to sleep, while she lay awake in misery and heartache.'[33] There we see the full cost of forgiveness being

---

**31** M Bordeaux, *Risen Indeed* (London: Darton, Longman and Todd, 1983) pp 89–90.
**32** W H Auden, 'The Sea and the Mirror' in W H Auden, *Selected Poems* (London: Faber, 1979) p 137.
**33** A Bridge, *One Man's Advent* (London: Fount, 1985) p 3.

paid; but it does not lead to a reciprocal putting to death of the sin in repentance. What can at least be said is that, despite the pain (or perhaps because of it) the mother is in a better position than if she had withheld forgiveness altogether. For that would have been to shut the door on the possibility of healing and to retreat, like Antonio, into lonely resentment, 'By choice myself alone.'

## Confession

Confession can play a vital role in the process of repentance and forgiveness, as Psalm 32.5 and James 5.16 suggest. When sin is confessed to God, or to another Christian, or to the offended party, responsibility can be taken for it and the demons of guilt and isolation and self-deception can be brought out into the open and exorcized.[34] It is characteristic of sin that it hates to be made public. It prefers to dwell in the dark corners of the human heart where it can remain secret and unacknowledged and where its grip is strongest. By failing to confess our sins we fail to be open with God, with ourselves and with our fellow human beings. It impairs our relationships and our self-knowledge.

Confession, on the other hand, involves coming to terms with the past and with our distorted or selective memory. It is in my memory that my own unique experience and story is stored. My identity, my self, is bound up with my memory, as Augustine explored at length in his *Confessions*: 'In the vast hall of my memory...I meet myself and recall what I am, what I have done, and when and where and how I was affected when I did it.'[35]

Where my memory is of sin and broken fellowship, the result is a personality which is to some extent distorted and impaired, often involving a reluctance to come to terms with the full extent of my sin. Part of the process of forgiveness must therefore have to do with the healing and restoring of memories by bringing them out into the open where they can be acknowledged and owned. As Rowan Williams argues, 'the word of forgiveness is not audible for the one who has not "turned" to his or her past; and the degree to which an unreal or neutralized memory has come to dominate is the degree to which forgiveness is difficult.'[36] He goes on to point out the impossibility of forgiveness for those whose crimes are so great that the memory has 'neutralized' them. Such was Adolf Eichmann who apparently blotted out his crimes from his memory and so was unable to come to terms with them later. Repentance is impossible if we cannot, for whatever reason, acknowledge the sin for which we are responsible.

**34** On confession to another, see Grove Spirituality 50, Mark Morton *Personal Confession Reconsidered* (Nottingham: Grove, 1994)
**35** St Augustine, *Confessions* (Oxford: OUP, 1991) p 186.
**36** R Williams, *Resurrection* (London: Darton, Longman and Todd, 1982) p 21.

The mere articulation of memories of sin and failure does not by itself lead to forgiveness. It is the confession of sin to the risen Christ, or to the fellow Christian (as a representative of Christ) that brings healing. In John 21 Jesus painfully reminds Peter of his denial of Jesus, not in order to exploit his moral advantage and crush Peter with guilt and despair, but in order to bring his exile to an end, to help him acknowledge the past and take responsibility for it, so that he can be restored to fellowship and have his vocation reaffirmed without any trace of self-deception or unreality.[37] Peter receives his apostolic commission not as a faithful follower of Jesus and saint, but as a repentant betrayer. As such his future ministry is built upon a firm foundation, because Peter knows from experience that he can never fall beyond the reach of grace, and so he will be less likely to trust to his own limited strength.

So confession drags sin out from the dark places of the heart and exposes our withered memories to the restoring light of truth. It allows us to place ourselves in Christ's presence knowing what we are, and being willing for him to nail our sin to his cross. As Bonhoeffer put it, 'the expressed, acknowledged sin has lost all its power. It has been revealed and judged as sin. It can no longer tear the fellowship asunder. Now the fellowship bears the sin of the brother. He is no longer alone with his evil for he has cast off his sin in confession and handed it over to God. It has been taken away from him.'[38]

Such confession does not have to involve other human beings, but where the community dimension is ignored there is a risk of superficial repentance, like that of Antony Bridge's father, because it is so easy for us to confess our sins only to ourselves at the same time imagining that we are confessing to God. According to Bonhoeffer, 'Is not the reason perhaps for our countless relapses and the feebleness of our Christian obedience to be found precisely in the fact that we are living on self-forgiveness and not a real forgiveness? Self-forgiveness can never lead to a breach with sin; this can be accomplished only by the judging and pardoning Word of God itself.'[39]

**37** *Ibid*, p 35.
**38** D Bonhoeffer, *Life Together* (London: SCM, 1954) p 88.
**39** *Ibid*, p 91.

# 5
# *Conclusion*

In order to forgive, God enters our state of sin and exile so as to bring us home. The story of the incarnation is the story of forgiveness, as God seeks the response of repentance and faith and finally wins it through the passion and Pentecost. It is a supremely costly journey, and one which involves identifying even to the point of death with those who need to be reconciled. It is a journey in which Love confronts the estranged and Innocence confronts the guilty, not in order to gloat or condemn but to woo and to welcome.

The response of confession, repentance and faith entails its own perilous voyage; in one sense this too is a costly journey, involving painful self-discovery and hard discipline. Yet it is a voyage for which the passage has ultimately been paid and a safe anchorage guaranteed. The experience of forgiveness with God is supremely an experience of freedom: freedom from the tramlines of past failure, freedom from fear of the future, freedom from the isolation of pride. Yet forgiveness is not just freedom *from*, it is also freedom *for*: freedom to take risks for God, freedom to offer ourselves for others, freedom to become forgiving. It is at that point, where those who find freedom can unlock dungeons for others, that we see the outworking of forgiveness.